WEST END

WEST END
A Sunken Village

Alastair Laurence

First published in 1992 by
Smith Settle Ltd
Ilkley Road
Otley
LS21 3JP

© Alastair Laurence 1992
Illustrations © The Copyright Holders 1992

ISBN 1 870071 89 1

British Library Cataloguing-in-Publication Data:
A catalogue record for this book is
available from the British Library.

Designed, printed and bound by
SMITH SETTLE
Ilkley Road, Otley, West Yorkshire LS21 3JP

CONTENTS

ACKNOWLEDGEMENTS

The author is grateful to Ethel Peel for allowing a selection of her notes on West End to be used as the appendix to this book. He also wishes to thank Jean Nossiter, Maurice Turner and Mark Whitley for checking his draft manuscript and making helpful observations and suggestions. Photographs which appear in the following pages have been generously provided by: George Brockhill; Gordon Cooke; Joanna Dawson; Hugh Hannam; Harrogate Museums; Jessie Heaton; Leeds Sailing Club; Jean Nossiter; Ethel Peel; Richard and Prue Towers; and Yorkshire Post Newspapers. Further thanks are owed to Bryan Brown for assistance in photographic work. The pull-out overview of West End by Chris Broughton has been specially commissioned by the publishers, Smith Settle Ltd.

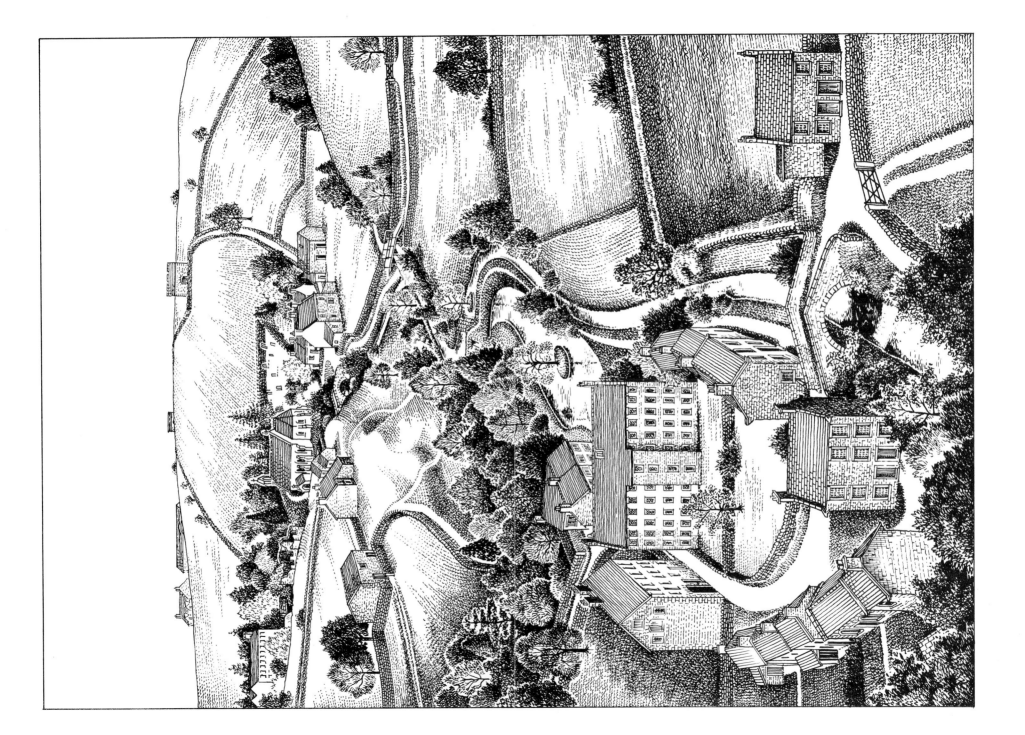

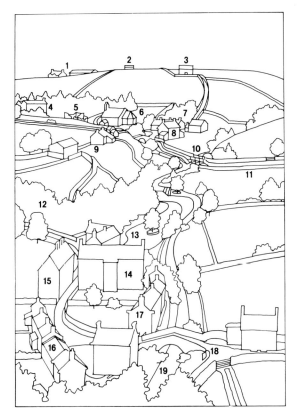

West End looking upstream circa 1875. A reconstruction based on old photographs and maps by Chris Broughton.

1. Whitmoor Farm
2. Miles Field Lair
3. High Lair
4. Patrick's Little Mill
5. Ruins of Patrick's Big Mill
6. Holy Trinity Church and Graveyard
7. Low Green
8. Post Office
9. Gibb House Farm
10. Meeting of the waters at Beckfoot Bridge
11. Scot Lane
12. Breaks Gill
13. Walker's Mill Dam
14. West End Mill (Walker's Mill)
15. Warehouse and Tenements
16. Primitive Methodist Chapel
17. Mill House
18. Street Lane Bridge
19. River Washburn

Introducing West End

'West End in the township of Thruscross in the parish of Fewston in the Forest of Knaresborough in the county of York'. So wrote Stephen Hudson, a native of West End, in the year 1786. His precise if somewhat pedantic definition of where he stood in the world is still helpful to us today. It reminds us that the hamlet of West End on the River Washburn, a locality within the enormous moorland township of Thruscross, possibly gained its name because it once lay towards the west end of the huge and sprawling Forest of Knaresborough. It also lay to the west of what is believed to have been the original centre of Thruscross: the interesting triangular Thruscross Green.

As a result of its extreme remoteness, West End remained an obscure backwater until well into the twentieth century. Matters were not helped by the fact that from the 1840s onwards the local population began to decline rapidly in numbers, the result of the collapse of the local textile industry. The district was inaccessible by rail or bus before the days of the car. For those few enthusiastic hikers, bikers or horse riders who managed to reach West End from the cities, the area became known as the 'Deserted Village' on account of its scattering of empty and derelict buildings.

This long-standing obscurity came to an end in the middle of the 1960s. Suddenly, as a result of media attention at that time, Thruscross became the best-publicised bit of the Yorkshire Dales. It had become widely known that this part of the Washburn Valley, including the hamlet of West End, was destined to vanish under the waters of a proposed new reservoir. Thousands of visitors now flocked to the Washburn, some to pay their last respects to West End, others to share in the general nostalgia and sadness which was felt by the local inhabitants; but most came out of sheer curiosity, to see for themselves the beautiful and lonely district they had read about in their newspapers and to observe the gigantic mass of concrete, Thruscross Dam, in course of construction.

When the dam outlet gate was ceremoniously wound shut on the 7th September 1966, and the waters of the Washburn slowly began to rise and lap around the foundation stones of the church, many people thought they had seen the last of West End. This was not to be so. Twenty-five years later, the extreme droughts of the summers of 1989 and 1990 reduced the water level at Thruscross to such an

The Rocking Stone.

extent that the original channel of the river was once again discernible and the ruins and foundations of old West End were exposed. Renewed media interest resulted in an upsurge in the number of visitors to the site – people who were curious to see what was left of the church and the stone river bridges. Many new visitors were frustrated by being unable to know 'what was what' as unfamiliar landmarks reappeared on the valley floor. One of the purposes of this book is to acquaint the reader with all those features which were, and to some extent still are, the essential West End.

Moorland

The dominant feature of West End landscape is rolling moorland. In winter this can be inhospitable and depressing; in summer, the moor's sombre solitude can be a refreshing tonic for the jaded city dweller in need of time and space for reflection and contemplation. West End is locked in by moor, or former moorland, on every side. To the west is the wild expanse known as Rocking Moor, in the middle of which is the Rocking Stone, close to the strange, stone-built hunting lodge. The Rocking Moor is accessible by footpath, and a rough cart track leads pedestrians up to the intriguing rocking stone itself, although visitors will be disappointed to discover that the stone itself no longer rocks, and hasn't done so for over 150 years.

To the south of West End is another moor, the Hanging Moor. Travellers here in the earlier years of the present century may have called at the nearby public house (now demolished) known as the Gate Inn, the curious sign of which was a small farmgate suspended from the branch of a nearby tree. The word 'hanging' in the context of the moor comes from the old English word *hangra*, meaning a steep, usually wooded, slope. This has nothing to do with a hanging farm gate! The confusion probably arose from the local road name, 'Hanging Gate', the word *gate* being Old Norse for 'way'; and so the way to the wooded slope became mis-translated by some ancestral publican to become a humorous and memorable inn sign. Attached to the gate in question was a quaint announcement:

> *'This gate hangs well and hinders none,*
> *Refresh and pay, and travel on.'*

Immediately north of West End are two further lumps of moorland. The first, Whitmoor, leads on to Hudstorth; and the second, Roundell's Allotment, is a tract of 431 acres of open land so named because the Reverend William Roundell purchased it around 1778 when the former Crown lands of the Forest of Knaresborough were sold off. The ruinous but still imposing Holmefield House, overlooking West End, was in all probability built by the Roundells as a hunting lodge attached to their adjacent moorland, just as the sentinel-like Rocking Hall is believed to have been erected by the Nicholsons for the same purpose on Rocking Moor.

Streams

Descending from the moorlands around West End is a bewildering jumble of streams and becks, most of which begin their courses in featureless waterlogged hollows. These watercourses have names, ranging from the prosaic-sounding Green Syke at Bramley Head, to ones with more interesting and unusual names such as Slush Dyke and Crackling Syke. All of the water courses end up in the River Washburn. The major tributary stream is the Capelshaw Beck, running eastwards off Rocking Moor. Before the construction of Thruscross Reservoir, the Capelshaw's confluence with the Washburn was at a most delightful and picturesque spot, known as Low Green or Waterhouse Green. Today, Low Green lies deep under the waters of the reservoir.

Towards the end of the eighteenth century, the potential of these streams for driving water wheels for industrial purposes soon became

The ruins of Holmefield House, West End.

recognised. By the early 1800s, a complex series of dams and goits had appeared on Capelshaw Beck to drive the wheels of no less than three newly-erected mills. Further downstream on the Washburn itself, a fourth mill had been constructed in the centre of West End. The earliest-known main activity of these four premises was the spinning of cotton yarn; but a general change-over to the spinning of flax for linen yarn had taken place by 1814.

As a result of all this new textile activity, the population of Thruscross soared to reach a peak of around 600 folk during the first three decades of the nineteenth century. However, most of the water-powered industry in the valley was to have a lifespan of little more than forty years. Competition from steam power, combined with the remoteness of the Washburn mills from the main commercial centres, caused them to die an early death, with very little local industrial activity taking place after 1840. A large proportion of the local population vanished in search of work elsewhere, houses became uninhabited and derelict (the census return of 1851 lists over thirty houses as unoccupied) and West End soon earned its reputation as the 'Deserted Village'. Robert Myers, a local gamekeeper, pinpointed the district's commercial problems when he wrote in 1906 that 'West End – is rather a wild part, and hard to get to'.[1] A more detailed description of the rise and fall of West End textiles is given further on in this account.

One of the features of Washburn water is its distinctly soft character, unlike the bulk of the waters flowing through the Wharfe Valley to the south. As a result, the water was very attractive to those intrepid plumbers and engineers engaged by the Corporation of Leeds to seek out and find new sources of water supply for the city. In particular, the softness and 'brightness' of Washburn water was a highly desirable asset for use in the woollen mills in and around Leeds. In 1852, the civil engineer J W Leather waxed lyrical on the subject:

'There are streams in the upper reaches of the Washburne, springing entirely from the Millstone Grit, which would defy competition from any quarter – [such] as the Thackray beck, the Hall beck and Redshaw Gill beck, and others – which yield large quantities of the most beautiful pellucid water.'[2]

Leeds Corporation's thirst for more abundant and better supplies of water ultimately led to most of the Washburn Valley coming into their ownership by the powers of compulsory purchase. There had always been plans, from the mid-nineteenth century onwards, to develop a storage reservoir at Thruscross as and when needed. The purchase of property at West End for this purpose eventually took place under the terms of the Leeds Corporation Act of 1897. However, over sixty years were to pass before the final decision was made to construct the massive dam at Thruscross and drown a large part of the locality.

Roads, Bridges and Fords

The two roads which today serve Thruscross run their parallel routes northwards from the main Skipton-Harrogate highway. The more interesting road of the two is the one at the west side of the valley, which winds past Blubberhouses Hall, crosses over Redshaw Gill Beck by a steep descent at Nethernooks Bridge, and continues up-valley past Cockber Bank to reach West End. In 1826, this stretch of lane was known as the highway from Appletreewick to Otley. A modern road (1966), branching off to the right shortly before Breaks Fold, leads directly down to the reservoir and crosses over the top of the dam. Three further roads, also branching off to the right (Breaks Lane, Corkscrew Lane and Clogger Lane) were severed when the valley was flooded. Now they lead nowhere – except to the reservoir edge.

The way up the east side of the valley is straighter and more uniform in character than that on the west. It climbs through the hamlet of Hardisty Hill and after about a mile the well-known landmark of the Stone House Inn appears at the crossroads. This section of the highway is named as Greenhow Hill Road or Sandygate. It was an important thoroughfare for farmers of former times, because they used it to carry quicklime from the kilns at Greenhow down to their fields at Blubberhouses, Fewston, Norwood and elsewhere in the lower valley. The Stone House Inn is believed to take its name from the fact that all the floors in the house, including the bedrooms, were at one time stone-flagged. Farmers using Greenhow Hill Road to transport lime would regard the Stone House as a convenient stopping-place for refreshment, and Will Abbot, a noted former publican here in the mid-nineteenth century, would sell home-brewed ginger ale at twopence a pint. It was a common sight to observe as many as fifteen carts lined up alongside the road when farmers called in for a drink.

The road which used to pass through the centre of West End is known as Street Lane. This thoroughfare traverses the valley on a north-east/south-west axis. Its importance in former times lay in the fact that it was the main route to Skipton, and so from the late eighteenth century it would link up to the Leeds-Liverpool Canal, and in the next century it would be the important connection to Skipton railway station. When the valley was flooded for Thruscross Reservoir, a half mile stretch of the lane was re-routed across the top of the dam.

Descending from the Stone House Inn, Street Lane has a number of noteworthy features along its route. Immediately above Ratten Row, on the right hand side of the lane, is a small outcrop of gritstone boulders, believed to have been known as 'Mawkin Cross'. Ratten Row itself, a group of houses alongside the lane, is recorded as 'Rattenroe' as early as 1686. Whether these were indeed 'rat-infested houses', as the name suggests, is open to question! It seems more likely that the name has something to do with the 'retting' stage (the soaking of flax fibres) during linen manufacture. The abundance of good springs and wells which occur in the vicinity would have been invaluable for this purpose. Towards the bottom of Ratten Row stood the Gate Inn previously mentioned.

Passing downhill next to the Gate Inn, Street Lane used to cross the Washburn by way of an old stone bridge; and it was in and around this bridging spot that the main centre of West End existed. Surrounding the bridge, on both sides of the river, were a dozen or so cottages, most of them built in the early nineteenth century when local textiles were booming. Near the bridge stood the Primitive Methodist Chapel, founded in 1829 and one of two Methodist meeting places in Thruscross. Opposite the chapel, on the north side of the lane, the tall and imposing West End Mill dominated the riverside landscape. Complete with its large adjoining pond, the mill dated from around 1791 and was erected alongside a much older township cornmill. The whole of this part of West End – the mill site, dam, bridge and the area covered by the cottages and chapel – disappeared from view once Thruscross Dam began to function.

Street Lane used to continue its progress cross-valley by climbing up the narrow nook in the hillside called Breaks Gill, until the road twisted and turned into Breaks Fold. This farm almost certainly takes its name from an old West End family, the Breaks, living here during the sixteenth and seventeenth centuries. From the mid-eighteenth century, the Fold was the home of the Horsmans for five generations.

After passing through Breaks Fold and crossing the Otley-Appletreewick road, Street Lane headed for the rougher lands of Rocking Moor to leave the township by way of the Turwath, a ford crossing Redshaw Gill Beck. This particular spot was important to local farmers for many generations, as the ford in question was their 'sheep dip' and a popular gathering place for flocks and families at sheep-dipping time in the summer months. The meaning of the name Turwath is likely to be 'Thor's ford'. A Viking shepherd who centuries ago gave his name to this ford may have been the same hill settler who erected some kind of stone standing landmark in the district: Thor's cross.

There is another former West End thoroughfare which needs to be explored. This is Scot Lane. Retracing our steps to Ratten Row, we discover a right turn at the bottom of the row which is now a gated cul-de-sac to the sailing clubhouse. Here was once the continuation of Street Lane down to the river bridge. A few hundred yards further along the cul-de-sac, near the present clubhouse, there was a fork in the road and Scot Lane branched off to the right. This obscure rustic way descended to the 'meeting of the waters' – the confluence of the Washburn with Capelshaw Beck. Here, Scot Lane crossed the river at Beckfoot Bridge. Pedestrians could use the narrow plank bridge, but farm carts, tractors and motor vehicles had to negotiate a ford. The origin of the name 'Scot' is uncertain. Early Ordnance Survey maps of West End show a point in Scot Lane marked 'Scot's Grave', lying a few hundred yards above the river. Whether this was indeed the grave of an unknown Scottish person, we have no way of knowing.

Across the water, the destination of Scot Lane was Low Green or Waterhouse Green, an area of flattish land at the confluence of the two streams. This part of West End had associations throughout most of the nineteenth century with the Patrick family, proprietors of two nearby textile mills. It is likely that the Patricks were responsible for constructing most of the hamlet of houses and cottages in and around Low Green, although the place had been the site of human habitation for centuries before. Low Green was a particularly favourable spot from the point of view of agriculture. The soil was level and deep, and the site was south-facing and sheltered. Significantly, Low Green was possibly the only piece of freehold farmland in the whole of the upper reaches of the Washburn Valley, the remainder of the land being copyhold and held under the constraints of the customs of the manorial court at Knaresborough Castle. Low Green was a noted watering place as well. John Walker Patrick, writing to his brother James from Low Green in November 1864 stated:

'I do not like to have to leave my old house at the Green where I have lived 24 years to live anywhere else, as the Green is so well watered. They fetch water from it to many places.'[3]

The quality of Low Green water, whether from small springs or from the two main watercourses, had obviously been long recognised.

In early 1938, Low Green was visited by the journalist Walter Thackray, who wrote the following entertaining account in the *Wharfedale and Airedale Observer* shortly afterwards:

'I entered a house at Low Green, and was invited to a cup of tea. The home is most unique, the lady having a partiality for clocks, of which I counted 23 of all kinds. The task of winding them up must keep one person fairly well occupied. Three wireless sets were to be seen, and attached to one I saw a clock. A gifted woman, with a remarkable power over birds, a robin is her daily companion, while budgerigars, canaries, linnets and goldfinches when released from their cages, will perch about her person. A friendly owl resides in the chamber. When liberated it flew to the woods, but returned to the hand of its mistress. Pigeons that fly up and down the Washburn Valley in flocks will gather on the top of an outhouse at her appearance, and will perch on her hands, and about her, to be fed.'

(The Lady whom Walter Thackray met was Mrs Ellen Waite, who was to die in 1953 at the age of sixty-nine.)

On the west side of Low Green, a few hundred yards further up the Capelshaw Beck valley, stood Holy Trinity Church. An ecclesiastical building had existed on this site from at least the mid-sixteenth century, the earliest known edifice being a small chapel of ease for the benefit of Thruscross residents, saving them the weekly three mile trudge down-valley to the parish church at Fewston. It is likely that the church was sited on this particular spot because it was a

The Meeting of the Waters at Beckfoot Bridge, West End.

Low Green, bridge and cottage, around 1930.

convenient central position in the middle of Thruscross township. In 1873 the church was rebuilt and a walled graveyard added. Access to Holy Trinity Church could be gained by a choice of three routes: Clogger Lane and Corkscrew Lane led down from the Otley-Appletreewick Road; and the previously mentioned Scot Lane was the access for residents from the eastern side of the valley – from Thruscross Green and Ratten Row. Like other groups of buildings at West End, the hamlet of Low Green slowly began to vanish from sight as Thruscross Reservoir filled up in the autumn of 1966.

Farms and Families

There used to be two very distinct and contrasting types of land ownership at West End. The first type consisted of the large areas of open moorland, which had come into the possession of a variety of wealthy absentee landlords during the second half of the eighteenth century. Each of these landlords had extensive areas of wild heath, with one or two small upland farms and gamekeepers' cottages attached. The chief function of the land was to provide sporting recreation during the shooting season. We have already noted the Rocking Moor, once owned by the Nicholsons of Roundhay Park, Leeds. Since the 1860s, this 2,500 acre area has formed a part of the Duke of Devonshire's Bolton Abbey Estate and it still fulfills the same role as it did over 200 years ago: namely, the provision of exclusive shooting facilities for a wealthy absentee owner and his circle of friends. The prosperous Roundell family of Gledstone-in Craven had considerable acres of sporting moor to the north of West End; and the Hanging Moor, further down-valley, once belonged to the Shann family of Tadcaster, affluent surgeons who had ecclesiastical links with Hampsthwaite and the vicarage there.

In complete contrast, the lower-lying lands of West End were divided up into a large number of smallholdings, held by copyhold tenure under the manorial court of the Forest of Knaresborough. This very different kind of land ownership was in the hands of a group of long-established local yeoman families, who were fiercely proud and independent but often impoverished. Most locals either had a very tough time of it trying to scrape a bare living off a few inches of indifferent soil, or they supplemented their meagre agricultural income with a useful trade. The Horsman family of Breaks Fold, for instance, were in the eighteenth century involved in the skinning of hides as well as cultivating their lands; and the Peel family of Cockber Bank below West End subsisted on their little fourteen acre smallholding for three

Holy Trinity Church, Thruscross.

or more generations, but their chief income must have derived from the trade of carpentry. At some date they also kept a beerhouse on the farm, known as the Dressers' Arms. Throughout the seventeenth and eighteenth centuries, the Hardistys had a smallholding of some thirteen acres of quite reasonable land near the river bridge in Street Lane, but additional earnings came through their ownership of West End cornmill which served the whole township of Thruscross. The Wigglesworth family of Thruscross Green, who held perhaps the largest smallholding at West End, nevertheless supplemented their income earlier in the present century by running a small village store in Scot Lane. For three generations they also provided a haulage and transport service to and from Otley. The Wigglesworths had long been the local 'Forest Constables', a supposedly hereditary office which may have dated back to the time of the family's local origins at Padside Hall in the early seventeenth century. Members of the family continued to hold office until the Forest Constables were disbanded as a body in 1916.

The exclusive group of rich moorland landlords played little part in the day-to-day life of West End, having very marginal involvement in local affairs. However, when called upon, they could be willing and sometimes generous benefactors. In 1826, for instance, Stephen Nicholson purchased a small piece of land at Whinney Hill and established a much-needed village school, subsequently known as the Rocking School on account of its moorland shooting connections.[4] Fifty years later, the Duke of Devonshire gave £300 towards the rebuilding of Holy Trinity Church (1873), his donation being six times greater than any other single subscription. At the same date the Reverend Danson Roundell donated the land for a new churchyard and provided a further £15, and Dr George Shann offered £10. Among the donations received from the local smallholders, John Moorhouse found 6d, and most others had difficulty in raising more than five shillings.[5] These very modest contributions did not arise because of meanness. Struggling in the face of chronic poverty, West Enders were proud to give to the church whatever they could realistically afford. Some of the farmers had strong Methodist loyalties as well, and so their financial support may have been committed elsewhere.

As an example of typical rustic frugality, we have the record of all the worldly goods and chattels of Godfrey Horsman of Breaks Fold, who died on the 23rd July 1841 leaving behind:

Purs	£4	2	0
Apparil	5	10	0
Bed, bedstead and bed close	5	15	0 [6]

Godfrey Horsman's son, Stephen (died 1878) was the last of the male line at Breaks. He was responsible for rebuilding a fair proportion of the farm buildings at the Fold during his lifetime. His descendants referred to him as 'great uncle Stephen, the strong man'. It was claimed that his phenomenal strength enabled him to lift 'a horse and a cart'. Whether he was able to carry both items at the same time remains a matter of serious doubt!

Among the other local families at West End, the Shepherds deserve special mention for their incredible continuity within the township. Their distant ancestor may well have been Richard 'Schiphird', listed in the poll tax roll of 1379. By the mid-1500s, William and Michael Shepherd and their households lived in the district. In the early eighteenth century, the family was based at Low Green. The house there in which Francis Shepherd dwelt had its rent allocated by Thomas Whittaker's trust deed (1729)[7] to charitable uses: in December each year, one third of the annual rent was paid to the poor of Thruscross, the remaining two-thirds being allocated towards the salary of 'the curate or minister of a certain chapel comonly called Westend chapel'. (This chapel was the forerunner of Holy Trinity Church.) Stephen Shepherd, a linen weaver of Low Green, made out his will in the winter of 1767, naming his wife Ursula, his daughter Mary and his sister Susannah. In 1829, Thomas Shepherd, also a weaver of Thruscross, is recorded as one of the founding trustees of West End Primitive Methodist Chapel. The last member of the family to live locally is believed to have been Stephen Francis Shepherd, who was buried in Holy Trinity graveyard on the 10th December 1921, aged sixty four.

The Garths were another typical West End family. Descended from Anthony Garth who lived towards the end of the eighteenth century, the family had a fondness for two unusual biblical names for their sons: Enoch and Elijah. There were no less than three Enoch Garths in the neighbourhood by 1840, as well as two Elijahs! For many years a line of the family resided at Whistle House, Whinney Hill, where Elijah Millard Garth had set up in business as the village shoemaker. Around the year 1938, Elijah's now elderly son and daughter-in-law, John and Sarah Garth, made a final pilgrimage to their ancestral home, by now in ruins.

One of the most well-known farming families at old West End were the Hannams. They were very much based at Bramley Head (a scattering of farmsteads higher up Capelshaw Beck Valley), where they inhabited Brays Croft, Cop Hurst, Summer House (High Lair), Lane Bottom and Croft House farms. One of their number, John Denbigh Hannam (1824–1906), was a generous benefactor towards

Elijah Millard Garth (born 1840)
and his daughter Maud.

the rebuilding of West End Church in 1873. As well as donating £20 towards the funds, he also gave a new stained glass window for the east end of the building, the theme of the glass being 'the Good Shepherd', and given in memory of his parents, William and Elizabeth Hannam of Brays Croft. Around the year 1901, John Hannam was forced by compulsory purchase to dispose of his farms at Bramley Head to Leeds Corporation. In a public-spirited mood, he had originally agreed to the sale in the understanding that a new and much-needed reservoir was shortly to be constructed; but he was very angry to learn after the sale that any new reservoir plans had been shelved indefinitely.[8] He must have been even angrier to learn that his powerful neighbouring landlord, the Duke of Devonshire, had not been required to relinquish an inch of land.

Sometime in the 1770s, a yeoman carpenter by the name of Robert Peel arrived at West End. He was the forefather of all those many Peels who have lived and worked in the Washburn Valley ever since. Robert was a native of Kildwick-in-Craven. He married a Washburn girl, Jane Wheelas, in 1777, and the young couple settled on a

John Denbigh Hannam (1824–1906).

smallholding at Cockber Bank where Jane's parents lived. On the 2nd January 1797, the Peels were able to purchase Cockber Bank from the landlords, the Reynards, and their descendants were to remain proudly independent here until the farm was compulsorily purchased, like the Hannam lands, around 1901.

George Peel, a wheelwright, and his wife Nancy represented the second generation of Peels at Cockber. Of their children, Samuel remained on the family smallholding until his death in 1905 at the age of seventy nine. When his property was in the process of being purchased by Leeds Corporation, a dispute arose as to its true market value. Walter Middleton, a land agent who had been called in as a result of the matter going to arbitration, made the following caustic comments about the Peels' property:

'The buildings are very dilapidated and will require the sum of £100 at least to be spent on them to make them tenantable. All of the water has to be carried from the field, some distance from the house. The road from the highway to the house is in a bad state. The trees by the house have been cut down, and the whole place looks as if the owner had starved upon it just as long as he could, and it is fortunate for him that the Corporation are taking it. The area of land is so small that it is impossible for anyone to make a living out of it. It is one of the most dilapidated farms in the Washburn valley.'[9]

Sam Peel's two younger brothers, John (born 1836) and Jesse (born 1839), were well-known and popular characters in the district. Both brothers kept public houses, John being licensee at the Gate Inn for a period of forty-five years, whilst Jesse brewed and sold ale at the Stone House for a fifty-four year span from 1868. John Peel was described by a contemporary as:

'. . . one of the most striking personalities in either the Wharfe or the Washburn valleys. When he had held the inn license for thirty years, a committee was formed to honour his long tenancy, and he was presented with a handsome timepiece, a pair of equestrian bronzes, a silver cruet, and a framed photograph of himself, bearing the names of the committee. He had a remarkable constitution. Right up to the time of his death he was accustomed to go out into the land in all weathers to attend to the cattle. Frequently he got soaked through, and it was his custom to sit over the fire until he got dry, or, if near bedtime he would throw his clothes off, and put them on again in the morning, still wet.'[10]

John Peel died in January 1923 at the ripe age of eighty-seven. His descendants still farm at West End: Richard and Isabel Peel and their family are based at Banks Farm, Thruscross Green; Geoffrey and Sylvia Peel and their family live across the valley at Lane Bottom Farm, Bramley Head; and Mrs Edith Townson (*nee* Peel) lives at Grey Stone Farm, Cockber Bank.

Jesse Peel, John's younger brother, was famous in his day as a brewer. Ale from the Stone House would be supplied by the barrel-load to the thirsty leadminers at Greenhow Hill. Jesse was also a noted musician, being skilful on both violin and cornet. He was leader of the Fewston brass band. It had become the custom to invite the band to head the procession at the annual Timble Club Walk. However, on one occasion, in 1858, the residents of Timble had for some reason decided to engage another ensemble, the Silsden band, who had duly arrived to perform on the day of the event. Much to everyone's surprise, Jesse and his loyal band of musicians suddenly appeared on the scene and, not to be outdone, they calmly took their place at the head of the procession. The dissonant clashes of the rival bands were afterwards long-remembered at Timble. While the Silsden band were concentrating their efforts into a delicate, lyrical ballad, Jesse's bandsmen would suddenly lurch into the rendering of a rumbustious march! For a number of years, Jesse Peel's bandsmen used to practice

John Peel of the Gate Inn (1836–1923).

in a room in a house in Ratten Row, although a neighbouring farmer complained that his cows 'went off milking' on practice evenings.

The remarkable life of John Demaine, a yeoman farmer from West End, was recorded by the local historian William Grainge in his *History of Harrogate* (1882). According to Grainge, John Demaine had reached the extraordinary age of 110 years at the time of his death in 1820. At the advanced age of ninety-seven, Demaine could still manage to hand-mow an acre of grass in a day, a task which was usually quite a challenge for a much younger person. When he reached his century, Demaine at last acknowledged that he was beginning to feel somewhat old, and bemoaned the fact that he could no longer leap the walls, hedges and ditches as he once loved to do. His favourite leisure pastime was to run after the hounds during a hunt, a pleasure which he enjoyed until the last five years of his life! Demaine's sight and hearing remained exceptionally good to the last. He died on a cold winter's day, 7th January 1820.

Jesse Peel's brass band outside the Stone House Inn.

The Textile Industry of West End

It comes as a complete surprise to many people when they are informed that the upper reaches of the Washburn Valley once had a large and thriving textile industry, based on four or five mills and employing hundreds of men and women. Today, hardly a single trace remains of these former hives of industrial enterprise. The foundations of three of the mills are submerged at the bottom of Thruscross Reservoir. Another mill higher up the Capelshaw Beck was burnt to the ground in 1838; and the derelict West House Mill at Fewston was demolished stone by stone to provide material for the new boundary walls of Fewston Reservoir.

The spinning and weaving of wool and linen had for centuries played a role in the economy of the Washburn Valley, although insufficient evidence survives to give us a clear picture of the exact

Stephen Hudson's house, West End.

nature and extent of the home-based enterprises. It is clear that those individuals whose livelihoods centred on textiles were among the most well off in the neighbourhood. The prosperity of the Robinsons of Swinsty Hall, for example, was probably based on the wool trade, and the family was running a 'shop' at the hall, complete with looms and spinning wheels, during the early seventeenth century.[11] Similarly, Richard Pulleyn who lived a few hundred yards to the north of Low Green, West End, was in possession of two looms, four pairs of shears, as well as spinning wheels and tenter frames at the time of his death in 1606.[12] Near the same spot 150 years later, the Shepherd family were busy making linen cloth on their home loom. Their contemporary, Stephen Hudson of West End, described himself as a 'shopkeeper', indicating that he was probably the proprietor of a weaving establishment. His elegant and stylish house, now unfortunately unoccupied and in poor repair, suggests that Hudson was a man

Street Lane Bridge, Walker's Mill and the former mill manager's house
(right). Photographed circa 1910.

of culture and affluence. The former nearby cottages would have been
occupied by Hudson's live-in weaving workforce.[13]

When the first of the big mills was erected at West End during the
1790s, its structure may have looked erratic and out of place in such
a rustic setting. Nevertheless, the mill's activities would have been
broadly familiar to many of the locals, and the pre-existing pool of
textile expertise in the valley may well have helped to get the new
enterprise off the ground.

From the surviving documentary evidence, it is apparent that one
individual more than any other was responsible for harnessing the
waters of the Washburn to turn water wheels: he was John Walker
of Otley (1756–1825). Walker was a newcomer to the textile industry
– his trade was that of silver plater – but he must have had
considerable financial means as well as a remarkable degree of
boldness to embark on his West End venture. He took into partnership
his brother-in-law Joseph Hardcastle, a grocer of Otley, and a certain
Richard Holdsworth, a wealthy maltster, also from Otley. The three
were joined by Robert Thompson, a joiner, and later by William
Maude, an ironmonger. On the 15th February 1791 the Otley
consortium bought from Samuel Hardisty of Thruscross for £530 the

The ruins of Walker's Mill, viewed from the top end of the mill dam.

old cornmill and millpond at West End Bridge. Shortly afterwards, they proceeded to erect a spacious textile mill on part of the newly-purchased site.[14]

The new mill commenced work with the water-powered spinning of cotton. In order to house the necessary workforce, the partners built thirteen cottages nearby. As the demand for cotton yarn increased, Walker and Company ambitiously decided to construct two further mills higher upstream, these being immediately to the west of the church on Capelshaw Beck. By the year 1805, Richard Holdsworth, Robert Thompson and William Maude had each withdrawn from the partnership. It is very likely that Thompson's role had been that of millwright. He was almost certainly involved in the initial setting-up of the wheels, machinery and internal joinery.

After 1805, John Walker and his brother-in-law Joseph Hardcastle were left in control of the business, Hardcastle being the 'sleeping partner'. Their foreman in the early 1800s was John Patrick, believed to have been a member of a Scottish family of 'Covenanters' who had settled at Felliscliffe. On the 1st June 1812, John Patrick married Walker's daughter Jane. This favoured position enabled him, nine years later, to purchase outright the two higher mills from John

The remains of Patrick's Little Mill.

Walker for the sum of £3,900. These premises were later to become known as Patrick's Big Mill and Patrick's Little Mill. One of the most memorable sights at West End during this period was the huge sixty foot diameter water wheel attached to the Big Mill. It is recorded that the wheel's axle alone was estimated to weigh five tons, and when it revolved to set the spinning jennies spinning, the whole fabric of the building rumbled and shuddered.

John Walker eventually retired to Otley, leaving his mill and ninety-strong workforce at West End in the hands of his only son, Charles James (1794–1875). By the year 1812, a fourth textile mill had become established at West End: known as Aked's Mill, the premises had been built around 1809 for John and James Aked of Halifax for the spinning of linen yarn rather than cotton. This building was sited even higher up the Capelshaw Beck valley, a field or so west of the highway at Dukes Hill. 'Aked's Dam', still marked on Ordnance

Creamware jug, inscribed: 'Charles Walker the son of John and Sarah Walker Westend Cotton Manefactors. May you never want a friend but happy may you be bleft with contentmen and from misfortuns free 1803'.

Survey maps, is to be found quite some way from the mill site and higher up the hillside. The premises founded by Akeds appeared to set a new trend at West End: by 1814, the other local mills had given up cotton spinning in favour of linen yarn manufacture.

We do not have sufficient information to pinpoint exactly when the decline of West End's mills began to set in. Things were certainly difficult during the few years immediately following the end of the Napoleonic Wars. Between 1815 and 1820, William Aked (one of the Akeds responsible for running the family mill) received financial assistance from Thruscross township funds. The money took the form of a loan to help maintain a number of young apprentices from valley families. They were named Robert Emsley, William Marjerison, Robert Peel, Sam Myers, Thomas Emsley, John Tuley, Joseph Young, John Hannam and H Throup. By the mid 1820s, Aked, now in serious financial difficulties and still owing the township £67, was faced with

Walker's Mill Dam, West End.

legal proceedings to recover the debt. However, in spite of their apparently weakened financial circumstances, all of West End's mills were able to keep ticking over throughout the 1820s and on into the 1830s.

The real crunch came with the year 1838, a sad year for Washburn textiles. The two Patrick mills lurched to a halt as a result of trading difficulties brought about by a serious slump. They were never to re-open for textile purposes. (For some years after 1838, the Little Mill functioned as a sawmill.) Aked's Mill, facing the same problems as Patrick's, suddenly burnt down in 1838. Naturally enough, claims were made that the fire was deliberately started in order to gain a desperately-needed insurance payment. As the families of West End witnessed the disastrous fire, they must have had the sickening feeling that any prospects of future employment and prosperity in the valley were now becoming very bleak.

Only Walker's mill survived into the 1840s. By this date, Charles Walker had withdrawn from active involvement in textile activities. He leased the mill to the trading partnership of Vipont and Whiteley, who continued flax spinning until they gave up around 1844. During the few years before this date, flax dressing, spinning and weaving had provided employment for over eighty of West End's residents. Two later tenants at the mill had brief and unsuccessful periods of trading: David Brown lasted barely a year (1846); and William Threlfall, who reintroduced cotton spinning, only lasted a span of three years until 1850. No new tenant could be found for the mill. The Washburn Valley now witnessed a rapid exodus of its unemployed and despondent textile workforce. The decade between 1841 and 1851 saw the population of Thruscross plummet by over forty per cent.

From 1850, Walker's mill stood empty and silent for a seven year span. Then in 1857, a small business known as Francis Thorpe and Company leased the premises in order to spin flax. Thirty-three textile workers found employment at Thorpes in 1861. In 1868, the mill was occupied by a new tenant, Thomas Gill, who introduced the spinning of 'heavy' yarns – hemp and jute for rope and twine making. Gill's activities continued on a modest scale, employing a handful of local people for a twenty year period until 1889. In that year, 'Tommy' Gill emigrated to New York – not New York, USA, but New York Mill at Summerbridge – where the close proximity of the Nidderdale branch railway was to be of far greater benefit to the company than the peace and solitude of West End.

With the departure of Gills, the textile industry of the Washburn Valley finally came to an end. In November 1890, the third generation of the Walker family tried to dispose of their West End property at an auction held by Messrs Dacre and Son at the White Horse Hotel, Otley. The starting price was £3,000, but not a single bid could be obtained. The old West End premises, by now something of a millstone round the necks of the Walker family, were unlettable and unsaleable. The fabric slowly crumbled into ruin, and the Walkers must have been grateful for the compulsory purchase by Leeds Corporation which came around 1901. Very little needs to be written about the sad ruins of the once-flourishing mill, apart from the observation that the derelict shell of the building was found to be useful for soldiers' target practice during the Second World War.

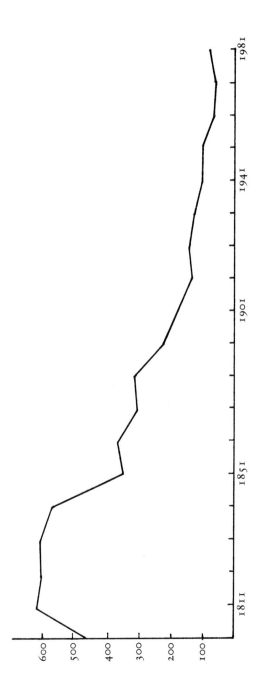

The population of Thruscross township, 1801–1981.

The Flood

Exactly 100 years before the wall of concrete at Thruscross began to stem the flow of Washburn water, plans were already being hatched in Leeds to create reservoirs in the valley. The Leeds Corporation Waterworks Committee had commissioned a report from their engineer, Edward Filliter, on 'the best mode of obtaining an additional and purer supply of water for the Borough of Leeds'. Filliter's report was dated the 11th September 1866.[15] Among his recommendations was the bold announcement that a chain of reservoirs should be placed in the Washburn Valley 'at and above Fewston, which will store the best flood and ordinary waters of the river and transmit them by conduit to Stubhouse Well and thence to Eccup'. Filliter went on to list no fewer than nine possible reservoirs in the valley: Lower Fewston, Upper Fewston, Thruscross, Capelshaw, Timble Gill, Hood-storth, Blubberhouses, Wydrah and Lindley Wood. Of these nine possibilities, the Lower Fewston was the largest, with a proposed capacity of 890 million gallons, whilst the smallest was Timble Gill, planned to hold 37 million gallons. Residents in the Washburn Valley would have been little relieved by Filliter's grandiose assertion:

'I do not propose to construct all these reservoirs at once, but as the Upper and Lower Fewston reservoirs, for storage and compensation respectively, would, with ease, enable you [the Corporation] to obtain 14 million gallons per day by gravitation . . . thereby doubling your present means . . . and carrying you on for probably twenty years to come, I consider that these would be sufficient for the present, and that the additional reservoirs . . . may be added when the occasion arises.'

Within a decade of Edward Filliter's momentous report, the construction of three reservoirs in the Washburn Valley was in progress. The 'Lower Fewston' reservoir (1876), known today as Swinsty, was completed along with its companion, 'Upper Fewston' (1879), now called Fewston. However, the Swinsty Reservoir was not destined to be a 'compensation' reservoir as originally proposed (the purpose of which was to maintain the volume of water in the lower course of the river to enable the cornmills at Leathley and Lindley to function unimpaired). This role was to be played by the third reservoir, Lindley Wood (1875), some way downstream from Fewston. The majority of the other reservoirs named in Filliter's original list of proposals never proceeded beyond the drawing board. Only Thruscross was to join the three originals of the 1870s, its role commencing (7th September 1966) almost 100 years to the day after Edward Filliter's report gave birth to the idea.

Holy Trinity Church, Thruscross.

The interior of Thruscross Church.

In June 1960, West End was visited by the then Minister of Housing and Local Government, Henry Brooke, who, accompanied by the local MP Sir Malcolm Stoddart-Scott, made a tour of inspection. During the course of their visit, a series of white markers were set up to show the extent of the flooding which would result from the intended reservoir, and flags were hoisted to indicate the alignment of the new dam. Shortly after the minister's visit (the purpose of which was presumably to give Whitehall's official blessing to the waterworks scheme), construction work commenced on the site.

In 1960, no family or individual was actually living below the proposed new 'water line', and so no eviction or re-housing of any kind was necessary. However, the matter of Thruscross Church was a sensitive issue. The site of the church at Low Green was a cherished beauty spot, the small rustic footbridge spanning Capelshaw Beck to reach the churchyard providing particularly fond memories of peace and tranquility for hundreds of former visitors. Most people could hardly bear the thought of such a unique and special place being lost forever. As the building and development of the dam proceeded, the small number of parishioners who continued to attend services at the church must have been constantly mindful of the fact that, within a matter of months, their long-established communal focal point would be engulfed by water.

The last service at Thruscross Church was held by candlelight on Monday 11th October 1965. On this occasion over 140 people came to share in a sad and nostalgic farewell. The church was packed to overflowing, and people without seats stood solemnly in the side aisle or remained in and around the entrance porch. As the strains of the last hymn died away and the last congregation dispersed, many of them tearful, Thruscross churchwardens were putting on a brave face and making future plans: the interior fittings of the old building – altar, pulpit, font and stained glass windows – were to be moved uphill a few hundred yards to a recently-completed replacement church, constructed by the Pateley Bridge builder Maurice Blades out of stones from the ruinous Walker's mill. Plans were also being drawn up to commence the gruesome but necessary task of exhuming many of the bodies in the graveyard and to re-inter them, along with all the old headstones, in a bleak and featureless spot at the side of Greenhow Hill Road. This arrangement of new church and new graveyard being widely separated on opposite sides of the valley was not a particularly satisfying solution; nor were the typical 1960s stark and mannered lines of the new church to the taste of the long-suffering local community.

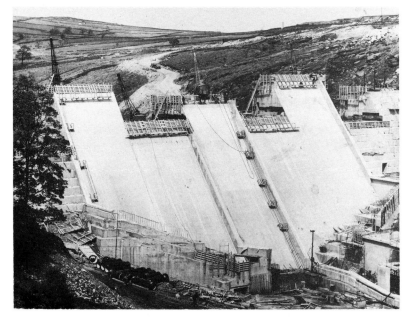

Thruscross Dam in course of construction, mid-1960s.

The old and now redundant church on Capelshaw Beck aroused a brief and final bout of newspaper publicity in the autumn of 1966, when the half-submerged edifice was visited by a solitary and unknown man, who, braving the cold floodwaters, swam out to the marooned roof of the church, on which he sat pondering for a time and enjoying what must have been a very curious sensation. At this particular date, the valley was undergoing a 'trial' flood. When the waters were let out after the test, a decision was made to demolish most of the church so that no part of it would be visible above the intended future water level.

Thruscross Dam was officially opened on Wednesday the 7th September 1966; or rather, the dam was officially 'closed', enabling the flood waters to rise. The ceremony was performed by Alderman J S Walsh, Lord Mayor of Leeds, accompanied by Alderman Sir William Hemingway (chairman of the Leeds Waterworks Committee) and Kenneth L Foster, chief engineer and head of the reservoir design team until his retirement in 1964.

Holy Trinity Church slowly disappears during the trial flood of autumn 1966.

To coincide with the ceremony, a number of concrete facts were made available: the Thruscross project represented five and a half years' work and cost about £1½ million. The newly-created sheet of water covered an area of 142 acres (58 hectares), the greatest depth of water being 120 feet. The holding capacity of the reservoir was claimed to be 1,725 million gallons with a reliable daily yield (via two huge 36″ diameter pipes) of 3,000,000 gallons. The majestic concrete

Sailing on Lake Thruscross.

dam stood 120 feet high and straddled across the width of the valley in an impressive 600 foot span. The contractors, Holland and Hannen and Cubitts Ltd, had managed to use up 186,900 cubic yards of concrete in the monolithic dam wall, the construction of which was supervised by project manager Barrie J White.[16]

As for the remains of old West End, most of the surviving ruins had been bulldozed flat in a short sharp exercise before the floodwaters rose. In the same operation, walls and fences were rapidly torn down, and all the trees standing below the intended water level sawn down to stumps. Only the stone bridges and the lower walls of Thruscross Church were allowed to remain standing, the site engineers deciding that it was not worth the trouble to completely demolish them. To this day, Street Lane Bridge, Clogger Lane Bridge, Thruscross Church footbridge and the remains of the old church itself still lie in the dark and mysterious depths of Thruscross Reservoir. The only visitors to the submerged ruins are the thousands of trout, introduced there by Leeds Corporation twenty-five years ago, who swim nonchalantly in and out of the rubbled remains.

Notes

Abbreviation: WYAS = West Yorkshire Archive Service

1. See Robert Myers' letter to Katherine Pulleine, reproduced in full in her book *The Pulleines of Yorkshire*.

2. Extract from the second report of J W Leather compiled for the Corporation of Leeds, February 14th 1852 (Leeds Reference Library).

3. Papers relating to the Patrick family of Low Green, West End, are to be found in Leeds Corporation Waterworks Deeds, bundles 793/1 and 793/2 (WYAS, Sheepscar, Leeds).

4. Stephen Nicholson's purchase deed dated 7th November 1826 is to be found in the Armitage papers, ref MD 279 (Yorkshire Archaeological Society, Claremont, Leeds).

5. See the published 'Statement of Receipts and Expenditure in connection with the Renovation of Holy Trinity Church, Thruscross', 1875; ref: Seal/A/3/4 (WYAS, Canal Road, Bradford).

6. The will of Godfrey Horsman of West End, yeoman, dated 25th January 1840, Knaresborough Wills (WYAS, Sheepscar, Leeds).

7. 7th March 1729: Thomas Whittaker of Black Hill in the parish of Skipton, mason, assigns property at Thruscross to trustees Robert Lolly, John Simpson, Stephen Gill, William Cockson and William Hardisty. Leeds Corporation Waterworks deeds, bundle 793/2 (WYAS, Sheepscar, Leeds).

8. Information received from Hugh Hannam, Harrogate.

9. Report and valuation of Walter Middleton, November 1901, Leeds Corporation Waterworks deeds, bundle 1591 (WYAS, Sheepscar, Leeds).

10. Notes in possession of Mrs Ethel Peel, Dacre Banks, Harrogate.

11. See the inventory of the goods and chattels of Henry Robinson of Swinsty, gentleman, 1639, printed in the Yorkshire Archaeological Society's record series, number CXXXIV (1972).

12. Knaresborough Wills (WYAS, Sheepscar, Leeds).

13. The will of Stephen Hudson of West End, shopkeeper, dated 27th June 1786. Knaresborough Wills (WYAS, Sheepscar, Leeds).

14. Papers etc concerning the Walker family and West End Mill are to be found in Leeds Corporation Deeds, bundles 1191/1 and 1191/2 (WYAS, Sheepscar, Leeds).

15. Edward Filliter: 'Report on the best mode of obtaining an additional and purer supply of water for the Borough of Leeds'. Waterworks Committee, Leeds, 1866 (Leeds Reference Library).

16. *Civil Engineering and Public Works* magazine, October 1966.

Appendix

Farming life at West End in the 1930s; the recollections of Ethel Peel

Ethel Peel (*nee* Garrett) was born at Bradford in 1908. She married the late Leonard Peel of Breaks Fold, West End, in 1934. (Leonard's grandfather, John Peel of the Gate Inn, is mentioned in the section on 'farms and families' in this book.)

It was in 1934 that I married and went to live in Thruscross. Fifty-seven years – but a whole world of change. Everything was done by horse power and muscle. There were no tractors, and few motor cars. All the farm work was done by means of horse-drawn implements. The blacksmith still spent his working hours shoeing horses and repairing farm implements instead of making fancy gates and railings. There were very few motor vehicles in West End at the time: only the vicar's (Mr Elliott), the Verity's, Mr Willoughby the Leeds Corporation land agent, and the carriers – Isaac Hannam and Robert Wigglesworth. Mr Hannam took his waggon to Otley Fridays and Mondays and to Pateley Saturdays. Mr Wigglesworth used his for delivering meal and grocery orders. On Friday he took passengers to Otley. On Monday livestock would be taken to the cattle market at Otley in his waggon.

A memory of farmhouses conjures up a stone-flagged kitchen with black-leaded grate (complete with side oven and boiler, reckons to hold kettles and pans), tabbed rugs, delft rack and 'wag on the wall' clock. Sitting rooms were oil-cloth covered, but again tabbed rugs – there was no electric for vacuum cleaners – and rugs could be taken out and shaken. There was no piped water in most farms, water being obtained by pumps or wells. Lighting was by means of candles and paraffin lamps. What a joy it was to get an Alladin or Tilley lamp with a mantle. With about two exceptions there were no bathrooms at West End; toilets were of the earth type, causing consternation and in some cases laughter from visitors from the city, the humour being at the sight of two and in some cases three holes of varying size on the well-scrubbed wooden seats.

The farms all had turbary rights on the moor, and each house had its peat and bracken stack. The bracken was used for bedding the animals and of course went back on the land in the form of manure. Coal was 15/- a ton delivered by a 3-ton lorry straight from the pit; but much peat was also burnt. The fire could be made up each night by placing the peat in good position, then by blowing with bellows each morning a good fire was soon going.

I had a small job attending to the water gauge in our front pasture. Each morning at 9.00am the water in the gauge was measured, the result put down in a book, and once a week the results sent off to the waterworks at Leeds.

The Stone family were good friends, and I shall never forget the kindness of Annie who invited me over and put me through my paces at pig-killing time. As a former city dweller, I had little knowledge of what was involved, but she showed me how to help with the scalding, rendering lard, dripping, craps, making brawn, stand pies, and what to do to put the meat in brine. There was very little surplus meat as it was customary to send gifts out to the neighbours. The menfolk attended to the salting down of the meat: one block and a half of salt, four ounces of salt petre and 2lbs of Demerara sugar was the amount used. After three weeks this was all rinsed off, and the meat set to dry on the hooks which could be seen in every house in the rural areas in those days.

No fields were re-seeded. Fields were occasionally changed over from pasture to meadow. There was much grazing of the 'Long Pasture', that is, the custom of tending cattle to allow them to graze the roadside verges. This was a time when farming was really at rock-bottom, before it was realised that we would need all the home food we could produce. There were no bulk sales of milk (this was before the days of the Milk Marketing Board). Artificial insemination was a thing of the future. We kept a bull and various neighbours would bring their heifers for serving. The cows were all horned, red and white Shorthorns, an occasional blue roan and a few Ayreshires. There were no Friesians or French beef types so prevalent today. Most farmers kept a cow or so for home use and to rear calves.

Milk was set up in milk bowls in the cellar dairy, left for a milking or so, then the cream would be skimmed off and the blue milk run off into pails. This was later mixed with meal and with the addition of hot water fed to the calves at blood heat. The cream was set up in a huge jar, stirred every day, then on Wednesday out was brought the huge barrel churn and churning would commence. This could go on sometimes for a long time before the welcome sight of the little butter grains appeared at the small window of the churn. Then the butter bowl and butter worker would be brought out and the butter washed, the churn milk run off (this would feed the pigs) and the whole of the butter would be washed, salted, worked again; then with the Scotch hands made up either into bricks of one pound or rolls of one and a half pound, weighed, stamped, rolled into butter paper and put in the big basket for the carrier to take to market.

A roll of butter 1½lbs was sold for 1/6d, the carrier receiving one penny for his services, so for all her work the farmer's wife received 1/5d. Eggs varied in price from as low as 9d to 1/6d or 1/10d per dozen, the carrier again making a charge for carriage. There was very little money at this time and the money received from the sale of eggs and butter would be housekeeping money for the week.

Farm rents were roughly £1 per acre per annum, 10/- for rougher land. Wages were approximately £1 10s per week. Young calves fetched £5, older ones £11 or £13; cows, £16; newly-calved heifers £22; sheep £1 5s or £1 15s according to breed; pigs about £3 for 8-week-old pigs; hens 2/6; pullets 4/-.

Going back to the eighteen-hundreds and early this century were the sheep washes. At Hudstorth and Turwath, families would gather together for the sheep wash. The whole family would attend and bring food, making it a great picnic. The custom seems to have died out in the 1920s. Perhaps the advent of compulsory sheep dipping with special detergent dips against sheep scab etc caused this. There are the remains of a concrete sheep dip at the bottom of Skaife Hill on the Capelshaw beck.

At Low Green near the Church lived Ellen and Will Waite. He was the church verger and cleaner. She was the lady noted for her large collection of clocks of all denominations. She had a wooden leg. Near to this house were several dilapidated cottages. One of these was known as 'The Postman's', where he sat to have his lunch. Jo Yates was the postman and cycled out each morning from Summerbridge, clearing mail boxes on his way home. He would bring back prescriptions from Dr Petch and any urgent requirements of shopping that were asked for. Mr Yates died in 1983 aged 97. An earlier postman was Bob Worthington who walked and who blew his bugle at Moorhouse Hill to alert the Valley of his approach. He was later provided with a bike.

Mr Wigglesworth who kept the shop in Scot Lane also sold provender. Fortnightly on a Tuesday all the Bramley Head farmers would gather on the green outside Lane Head farm with their horses and carts to meet Mr Wigglesworth and get their meal and groceries. Flour was bought by the 10-stone pack; wholemeal and oats etc also in large quantities, all homes having meal arks of some kind or another. Yeast was bought for a fortnight and the bread rose as well on the second week as the first. As most people had home-fed bacon and ham and produced their own eggs, lard, butter, preserves, potatoes, milk etc, the main groceries bought were flour, tea, sugar, salt, dried fruits, candles, soap and matches. Bread and cakes were all baked at home along with fruit pies and pasties. The shop in Scot Lane was later tenanted by Harold Murgatroyd.

There was a Mr Whittaker, cobbler and shoemaker, who came from Addingham at regular intervals. Our Bramley Head neighbours always came across to Lane Head farm in their clogs (wellies not having as yet reached West End). They changed into their shoes for going further afield.

There was also Johnny Myers, a Lancashire man who was the embodiment of all the pedlars. Travelling by bus from Skipton, walking from Kex Gill, he would arrive with two great baskets covered with America cloth. He stayed for a few days at Breaks Fold. After a good wash, a meal and pipe of tobacco, he would proceed to display his wares: buttons, pins, needles, reels of cotton, laces, studs, shaving soap etc. For the next few days he would go around the various farms and would be away from breakfast till dark. Anything could be ordered from him, and goods were always of the best quality.

Williams' Catalogue was a great stand-by, as few farmer's wives went to market each week, and many shopped by using this catalogue whereby goods could be ordered by post. Occasionally a neighbour would send off for a box of herrings or kippers and several families would help by buying a share.

Home remedies were used frequently for most kinds of illness and the doctor was called in as a last resort usually. The same applied to vets: things had to be woefully wrong before he was called in. Just prior to our marriage, my mother-in-law had suffered among her beasts an epidemic of 'pick', contagious abortion or brucellosis. Whatever name it was known by, it was a tragic matter and its effects were ruinous. The vaccination programme against this disease was just beginning and I remember our first heifer calves being vaccinated at a cost of 2/- per head. There was also a disease known as 'quarter felon' and a supposed cure for this was to insert a tarred rope into a beast's dewlap for a day or so. Whether this worked or not, I have no knowledge. Knowlson's 'Cattle Doctor and Farrier' was a great stand-by, recipes for stomach powders consisting of ginger, epsom salts and bicarbonate or soda prominent. Osmond's conditioning powders, Cataline Ovaltine, Elliman's horse linament and various other preparations were used.

Mr Joe Hannam who lived at Lane Bottom had various herbs in his garden, which were regularly purchased by herbalists from the town. Joe was a maker of besoms (heather brooms). He also entertained us by playing his concertina.

Just below the Gate Inn was the Red Well, which was supposed to have medical properties. People used the water to cure warts and wash 'sore eyes' – a thing we do not have today but very prevalent in the past. Old Will Nelson, an elderly neighbour of mine in the 1930s period, used to tell stories of the cures, one in particular of a small boy of four years old who had never walked. His mother was advised to tip him head over heels in the Red Well. After a few days of this treatment, he began to walk.

Cricket always had a following. When the Enclosure Awards were made, Thruscross had eleven acres of land on Thruscross Green allocated for a public recreation ground and sheep pen. Here the local teams played on land which would almost have served as a ski slope – none of our Yorkshire players would have wished to know it. It beat me how they managed to play on it, but matches were played Saturday afternoons and evenings. Then all at once the matches there ceased and the keen cricketers went to play on the lovely cricket ground at Blubberhouses which had been made for Colonel Galloway.

On Monday evenings in winter there was a club for the men, held at the Rocking School, where they played darts and dominoes. A similar club for the women folk soon folded up due to lack of support. At full moon in winter were whist drives followed by dances. People sat at the school desks to play whist. Supper would be served in the classroom, then with the seats placed back against the wall, the floor polished, and to the music of the piano played by Mrs Verity, Miss Foster or myself, dancing would go on until perhaps 2am.

They were great party-givers in the West End. Christmas-time parties went on well into January. I never saw any drinks at these parties except home-made wine. For some reason, this was thought to be non-intoxicating. Dandelion, cowslip, elderberry, rhubarb would be offered. Rhubarb had a kick like a mule and could knock strong men over. Ginger wine was more innocent. On leaving a party one would be offered a piece of rich Christmas cake and a 'glass of my home-made wine'. A custom which I enjoyed very much was that of 'setting': when leaving a house the host and hostess would say, 'We'll set you', and walk almost half-way home with the guest.

One evening in summer a young man called and asked to see the boss. He was in need of a bed for the night. We fed him, gave him bed, breakfast and a packed lunch for the next day. He was tramping from Scotland seeking work. I often wondered how he went on, and also if we would dare to do the same today.